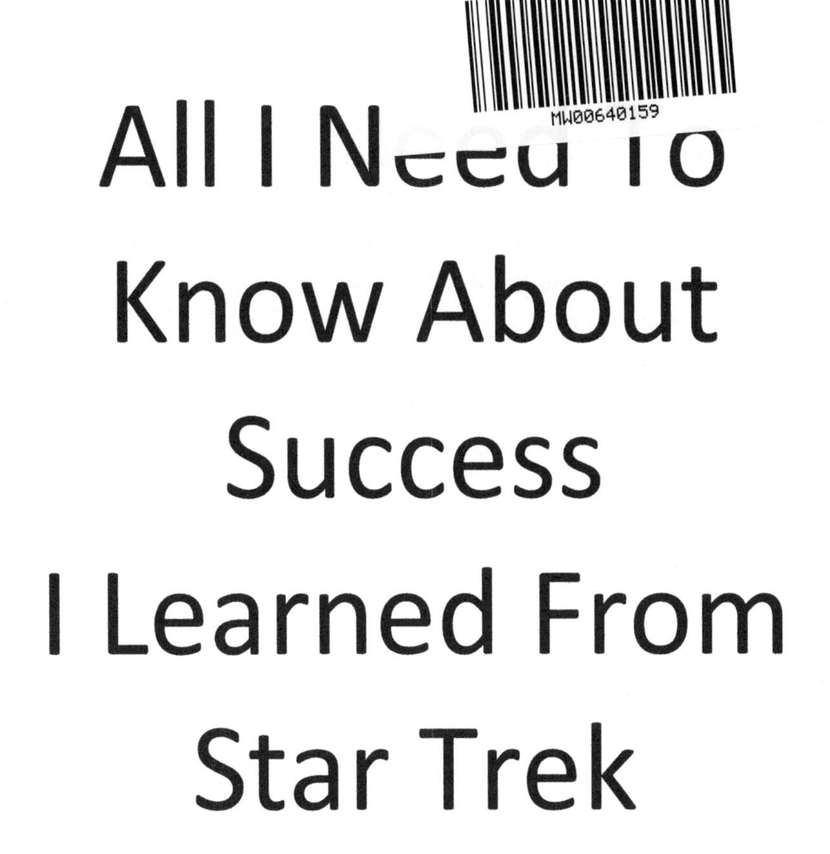

All I Need To Know About Success I Learned From Star Trek

Glen Henderson

Prominence Publishing
www.prominencepublishing.com

The author can be reached as follows:

Glen D. Henderson
1111 Brecon Hall Drive
Houston, TX 77077
glen.henderson@gmail.com

Cover photography by James Thew

All I Need To Know About Success I Learned From Star Trek/Glen D. Henderson. – 1st ed.

ISBN: 978-1-988925-71-4

Acknowledgements

My wife Paula, who, by her love and support and her personal example of excellence, inspires me every day.

My good friend and publisher Suzanne Doyle-Ingram, who FINALLY got me to go ahead and "write the damn book!"

My daughters Clare and Lizzie: may you reach your own stars.

So many leaders, coaches and mentors have guided and led me on my journey. Among them: Todd Falcone, Dr. Doug Firebaugh, Eric Worre, Kody Bateman, Bob Burg, Andrea Waltz, Richard Fenton, Alan Pariser, Norman Vincent Peale, Dale Carnegie, Napoleon Hill, Wallace D. Wattles, John Milton Fogg, John and Shannon Lavenia, John C. Maxwell, Dr. Ivan Misner, Ray and Jessica Higdon, and Zig Ziglar.

Foreword

Just reading the title makes me feel like I'm going on an adventure...

While I've never considered myself to be a die-hard Star Trek fan, as a youth I certainly had my share of time watching Kirk and company do their thing on the television. To this day, audiences young and old find entertainment in this ongoing tale of exploration into the unknown. It was only a matter of time until someone put down in writing the insights gained from the Enterprise's various exploits. While some are quite bizarre, they contain many lessons which can be applied to common life if we look deeper than mere entertainment.

Glen has done exactly that, extracting metaphors for successful living that everyone can relate to. From the objectivity and logic of Spock to the leadership, adaptability and intuition of Kirk, Glen points out lessons which are easy to apply. Entrepreneurs will find Glen's lighthearted approach especially pleasing, as he offers none of the unnecessary complications that other authors rely on to assert their own self-importance. You can save your copious note-taking for other books. Glen merely offers uplifting reminders of timeless principles as enacted by some of the most successful entertainers in modern history.

These are principles which are easily overlooked, as we are often so engrossed in our own drama that we neglect the art of observation. Eliminating doubt, maintaining your purpose in the face of adversity, recovering from misused and misdirected emotion, exercising your power of choice – these are beneficial conditions regardless of whatever worldly pursuit you're after (or whatever planet you're pursuing it on).

By finding small lessons embedded in fascinating stories we gain tools to overcome the trials we all face. Whether you're a Star Trek fan or not, I'm sure you can recognize times when you thought it would be wonderful to adopt the traits of some character on screen or on stage. From time to time I've entertained the idea of being completely impassive, logical and objective, like a Vulcan... and if I could choose such a thing, would I?

Regardless of who your "hero" is or what character you relate to (in Star Trek or otherwise), we all take cues from our environment which shape our perception and behavior. I can think of worse influences than that of the world Gene Roddenberry dreamt up. This is especially true in modern times, when much of pop-culture seems bereft of principles while pursuing self-interest at all costs ... actually, not unlike The Borg. "Resistance is futile - you will be assimilated." But I digress ...The virtues of being goal-oriented, taking risks, being consistent, learning from one's mistakes and developing persistence are as valuable today as they ever were. Perhaps Star Trek itself has persisted for generations because so many people have found meaning and guidance in the stories it contains.

As you read Glen's observations, see how you can apply them into your dealings with other Earthlings today, and on a consistent basis. The worst-case scenario is that you decide to binge-watch episodes of 1960's sci-fi. The best-case scenario is that you live long and prosper, while demonstrating to others how they can do the same whether they have pointy ears or not.

May the Force be with you.

Oh, uh, am I allowed to say that?

Whatever,

John Lavenia

Preface

Whether you're a Trekkie, a Trekker, or one of the many millions of people who grew up with the franchise...this book is going to take you on an entertaining and insightful journey with lessons on success...directly from the Starship Enterprise.

My good friend Glen Henderson has been a student of success for many years, and one of the most well-versed Star Trek aficionados I have ever met.

This book is filled with recaps of some of the best Star Trek episodes ever aired...all with incredible life lessons that can be applied in literally every area of your life. As Glen takes you through these life lesson episodes, you'll be able to take these learnings and directly apply them into your business and your life.

This book is filled with lessons on leadership, mindset, integrity, decision-making...and so much more!

And...the best part is, they're all wrapped up in taking you back inside the Starship *Enterprise*.

This is one of the most creatively written and entertaining books I've read in a while. And...I'm one of those guys that grew up watching Star Trek. I had NO idea that there were so many life lessons to be learned from a show I began watching in my earliest years!

Get ready and let the stories and the lessons unfold as you read this fun and entertaining book, *All I Need to Know About Success I Learned from Star Trek* by Glen Henderson!

Todd Falcone

This book is dedicated to the Captains and crews of the Starship Enterprise ... who taught a wide-eyed five-year-old kid to look up into the stars, and dream.

Table of Contents

Chapter 1

"To Boldly Go"

Space: The Final Frontier.
These Are the Voyages of the Starship Enterprise.
Its continuing mission:
To explore strange new worlds;
To seek out new life and new civilizations;
To boldly go where no man has gone before.

For more than half a century, these words have been ringing in the ears and thrilling the hearts of *Star Trek* fans around the planet.

In fact, it's probably fair to say that most *Trek* devotees could quote the mission of the *Starship Enterprise* from memory, immediately after being awakened from a deep sleep.

But what do these words *really* mean?

Are they anything more than just a cute opening line to a popular old TV show?

Do they have any application in real life?

And, most importantly for *our* conversation, what do they mean, or what could they mean, to someone seeking *true* success in their own life and work?

I've always believed that the words of the *Enterprise's* mission speak to the very heart of what it means to take on the grand adventure of building a career - and a life - you can be proud of.

If you've decided to embark on this mission with me, I believe, as the great network marketing trainer Eric Worre has said, that you are one of the "Smart Ones."

You can see a future that no one else can see.

Where others see hardship, you see challenge.

Where others see failure, you see opportunity.

Where others see the end of the line, you see the beginning of a journey.

Where others feel fear, and draw back, you feel fear - and step forward with your head held high.

You understand, as do James T. Kirk, Jean-Luc Picard, Benjamin Sisko, Kathryn Janeway, and all the captains and commanders and intrepid space-faring souls of the *Star Trek* universe understand ...

... one eternal, unchanging, exhilarating truth:

Beyond what you can see right now, beyond what you can understand at this moment, beyond the outermost limits of your comfort zone, there is a vast galaxy of knowledge, of achievement, of human connection, and of triumph over fear and misunderstanding and obstacles and anything else that stands between you and reaching your life's highest goals.

But, with apologies to the Chinese philosopher Lao Tse: the journey of a thousand light-years begins with a single step.

Let's take that first step together, by *setting our course.*

After all, if we don't know where we're going, we could end up, in the words of two famous *Trek* characters you'll soon meet, in a situation where we're *"pursuing a circular course ... and at Warp 10, we're going nowhere mighty fast!"*

Here's what you can expect as we journey together:

First: For our purposes, I will be focusing my attention on the first two *Trek* franchises, namely *Star Trek: The Original Series* and *Star Trek: The Next Generation.*

I have great respect and admiration for many aspects of all the other past and current *Trek* iterations (and who knows, you and I may be taking a look at some of them in the future – nudge nudge, wink wink).

That being said, these are the two franchises that I know best, so it seemed prudent to start with those that are nearest and dearest.

Second: We'll be looking at episodes, scenes, characters, conversations, and actions from both the television series and feature films of these two *Trek* franchises.

Third: Much of what I'm going to share will be intended primarily for entrepreneurs, small business owners, salespeople, and network marketing professionals.

Certainly these are not the only places in the world where success and achievement may be found; but many of the examples that I have personally seen and experienced arise from within these professions, so we will focus our attention here for now.

Finally, each chapter will lay out:

- The series episode or film in question;
- The characters involved and the situation;
- Selected dialogue and actions - who said or did what to whom and why;
- The deeper meaning and life principles I've gleaned; and finally,
- The leadership and success lessons I believe YOU can use.

If you're new to the *Star Trek* universe, I hope you'll come to realize, as I have, that *Star Trek* is more than just a TV show, more than just a movie:

It is, in many ways, a metaphor for life, an exploration of the human condition, and – if you're willing to look a little deeper and with an open mind – a guide to help you on YOUR journey aboard the third planet in our solar system.

If, like me, you're a lifelong fan, I hope you'll find this a delightful stroll down Memory Alpha Lane!

Who knows, you might even be shown a glimpse into a rich trove of truths you may not have seen the first time your mind's eye patrolled the bridge of the *U.S.S. Enterprise.*

Now then, our course is laid in, our engines are at full power – ready?

Here we go:

Ahead Warp Factor 9 - *engage!*

Chapter 2

"All Hands: This Is The Captain"

Franchise: The Original Series
Season 1, Episode 14: "Balance Of Terror"

I'm beginning with this as the first full episode we'll explore together, because it contains so many lessons on the nature and conduct of *leadership*. I've always believed that true success in any organization, be it a corporation, small business, nonprofit, network marketing, the military, the arts, or any other venture you might name, is driven first by a competent and confident leader. We'll examine this idea in later chapters, but here in this episode we're shown Captain James T. Kirk in one of his finest hours as a leader.

In all of Captain Kirk's interactions with his crew as well as with others, he exudes an inner calm and confidence, the result of his complete command of his own technical and tactical skills, as well as full self-awareness which allows him to monitor and control his emotional responses in this dangerous and high-pressure situation.

We're also going to see:

- Kirk's encouragement of differing opinions;
- His complete rejection of bigotry and race hatred;
- His demonstrated confidence in the members of his team;
- His willingness to accept full responsibility for his actions and their consequences;
- His reliance upon his friends and confidants for support; and
- His respect and graciousness, even towards avowed enemies.

Didn't know that you could find so many leadership lessons in one episode of a sci-fi series more than half a century old, did you? Well, here we go – "brace for impact!"

What Happens And What It Means:

As "Balance of Terror" opens, the *U.S.S. Enterprise* finds a group of deep-space outposts of her allied organization, the United Federation of Planets, under attack by a mysterious enemy.

(By the way, this is the first appearance in the franchise of the alien race known as the Romulans.)

The *Enterprise* moves to investigate and, if possible, protect the outposts; unfortunately, several of the outposts are destroyed before Kirk can move his ship into a position to help.

In pursuit of the enemy vessel, Kirk demonstrates a smooth working relationship and rapport with the members of his crew. He is able to communicate his wishes to his crewmen often with merely a word or a glance, as when he speaks with his chief engineer, Commander Montgomery Scott:

> *Kirk: "Scotty ..."*
>
> *Scott: "I've ALREADY talked to my engine room, Captain – we'll get more speed out of her."*

If you've ever had a relationship like this with a teammate or business partner - so coordinated, so in sync that you almost felt you could predict each other's moves - you know exactly how a scene like this plays out.

Once the Enterprise is within "sensor range" and detects the enemy vessel, Kirk's science officer (the legendary Mr. Spock - we'll learn MUCH more about him later on) manages to capture a video image of the Romulan ship and its commander. Much to everyone's surprise, the Romulan commander bears an uncanny resemblance to Spock!

Upon seeing this, the ship's navigator, Lt. Styles, is immediately inflamed with suspicion and hatred against Spock. You see, there had been a previous war between the Federation and the Romulan Empire, and several members of Styles' family had been killed in that war. Seeing the resemblance, he conflates Spock and his enemy. At one point, Styles, in an act of open disrespect and contempt, even mutters an insulting comment in the direction of Spock (who, by the way, is his *superior officer*) - but Kirk instantly shuts him down:

> *"Here's one thing you can be sure of, mister: leave any bigotry in your quarters – there's no room for it on the Bridge. Do I make myself clear?"*

Captain Kirk calls a briefing with his senior officers, to analyze the situation and determine how to proceed. During this meeting, Kirk continues to lead his team with a cool head and a steady hand, even in the face of disagreement and conflict. Viewpoints and opinions are bandied about back and forth across the conference table; even Styles (yes, THAT Styles) is invited by Kirk to speak freely (*"Go ahead, Mr. Styles – I called this session for opinions"*). Styles advocates for a direct attack against the Romulans, but he does it by again suspecting and accusing Spock of dual loyalties.

> *"These are Romulans! You run away from them and you guarantee war. ... Now you know that, Mr. Science Officer - you're the expert on these people, but you've always left out that one point. Why? I'm very interested in WHY!"*

Imagine challenging your boss's motives to his or her face, IN FRONT OF THE ENTIRE SENIOR STAFF.

Let that sink in for a moment.

But... it turns out that Styles is RIGHT. Even Spock (clearly demonstrating that he never takes insults personally) actually agrees with him.

The interesting part of this exchange, though, is that Kirk *allows it to continue.* He does order Styles to calm himself emotionally at one point, but he is clearly more interested in the *result* of this conversation than in its *form*.

The goal here is to *win*. If emotions run a bit high along the way, the Captain can manage that, and live with it ... in the service of victory.

(There's also small moment in this same meeting where Kirk gives a team member time to shine:

In planning their next move, Kirk brings up the possibility of using a passing comet as cover for an attack. He asks Spock about the comet, called Akaris 4, and hands him a reference book to use; Spock gently pushes the book aside and gives a complete description of the comet in question *from memory*. ... Give your people the stage and let them do what they do best. Nice.)

There comes a point in this episode when Kirk has to make a momentous decision, one that could cost millions of lives and trigger an interstellar war. How he handles that moment is instructive.

One result of the prior Romulan/Federation conflict was the establishment of a "Neutral Zone" between the two powers, as a kind of physical buffer to help prevent future hostilities. Entry into this Zone by either side would be considered an act of war.

As the *Enterprise* is pursuing the Romulan vessel, they draw ever closer to the borders of the Neutral Zone. Seeing no alternative if he is to defeat the Romulan commander, Kirk makes the fateful choice – notice how he phrases his order to his communications officer:

> *"Lieutenant Uhura, Inform Command Base: In my opinion, no option. ON MY RESPONSIBILITY, we are proceeding into the Neutral Zone."*

In his sober visage, the implication is clear: he knows EXACTLY what he is doing, and what it may mean for the fate of the galaxy. Yet he does not hesitate to make the command decision, and he willingly takes the full weight of that choice upon himself.

It's a simple statement, yet it's full of emotional power and courage.

Just before the climactic battle with the Romulan ship, Kirk has a moment of rest in his quarters. He is visited by his chief medical officer and close friend, Dr. Leonard "Bones" McCoy. In their chat before returning to the bridge, Kirk lets his guard down for an instant, and we see his inner misgivings;

"I wish I were on a long sea-voyage somewhere ... not too much deck tennis, no frantic dancing ... no responsibilities. ...

"I look around that bridge, I see the men waiting for me to make the next move ... and Bones, what if I'm wrong?"

Kirk doesn't really expect an answer – but Bones gives him one anyway. It's a deep expression of the bond between the two men. Read this once – no, twice – and ask yourself what you wouldn't give to be valued like this:

"In this galaxy, there's a mathematical probability of three million Earth-type planets. And in all the universe, three million million galaxies like this one. And in all that, and perhaps more, only one of each of us. ... Don't destroy the one named Kirk."

Friends.

Now then, as to the final battle ... wait, you don't expect me to actually give away the WHOLE episode, do you? THAT part, you'll just have to watch for yourself. About that battle, though, two comments.

First, during the cut-and thrust of combat, Kirk on several occasions recognizes that he is pitted against a cunning and shrewd adversary:

> *"He did exactly what I would have done – I won't underestimate him again."*

Ultimately, Captain Kirk and his crew do achieve victory over the Romulan vessel and its commander. The Romulan captain, whose name we never learn, demonstrates that he understands the respect, even in defeat, that he has been shown by Kirk:

> *"I regret that we meet in this way. You and I are of a kind; in a different reality, I could have called you friend."*

Even his enemies acknowledged James T. Kirk as an uncommon leader. I hope that you are beginning to get a glimpse of what he and his crew, and so many in the Trek universe, whose names are household words to those of us who grew up with them, have to teach us about leadership, personal growth, and the success that we all seek.

Leadership Lessons You Can Use:

- Encourage diversity of opinions, even when they differ from your own. Seek out robust debate.

- There can be no place for hatred, bigotry, or prejudice in the mind of a leader.
- Demonstrate your confidence in your team - give them room to shine.
- Take full responsibility for your own choices and the results of those choices.
- Find a few friends you can count on even in tough times.
- Show respect for everyone, even for adversaries.

Chapter 3

"The Smallest Doubt Would Be Enough To Kill You"

Franchise: The Original Series
Season 3, Episode 6: "Spectre of the Gun"

Entrepreneurs, salespeople, and network marketing professionals often speak of *mindset* as a key factor in their chances of success. Books have been written about it; speeches have been given to cheering crowds extolling its power; millions of dollars have been spent on training and coaching programs – all with one goal:

> *The cultivation of a frame of mind which can focus us on our goals, ignore rejection and criticism, and drive us without distraction or diversion toward our chosen destination.*

Here in "Spectre of the Gun," we'll take a look at an allegorical demonstration of this principle … one which, in this case, literally *saves the very lives* of our heroes.

Prepare yourself: we're about to take a trip into not only the function of the human mind, but into *Trek's* view of the very nature of reality.

What Happens:

Captain Kirk and the *Enterprise* crew have been dispatched on a diplomatic mission to establish relations with the inhabitants of the planet Melkotia.

As they approach the planet, however, they are confronted with a "space buoy" which transmits a threatening message, warning them to withdraw. Their message is delivered *telepathically*, sent so as to be heard in the native languages of each of the members of the bridge crew. (Keep this point in mind; it'll become important in a moment.)

It soon becomes clear that the Melkotians are xenophobes, desiring no contact with outside worlds. Of course Kirk, being Kirk, ignores the warning and proceeds with their mission.

Once Kirk, Spock, Dr. McCoy, Chief Engineer Scott, and the ship's navigator, Ensign Pavel Chekhov, "beam down" to the planet's surface, they are confronted again by the

Melkotian, who metes out punishment for their "disobedience."

Using the Melkotian telepathic power, he reaches into Kirk's mind and chooses an incident from Earth history as the "pattern" for their execution: The Gunfight at the OK Corral in Tombstone, Arizona on October 26, 1881.

As you may recall, on that date the Clanton Gang faced off against the Earp brothers, Tombstone town marshals, along with Doc Holliday. The Earps killed the Clantons that day ... and in this "pattern of their death," Kirk and his crew are now the Clantons.

As they move through the town, Kirk and his men are constantly addressed and treated by the townspeople as though they actually are Ike Clanton and his cohorts. No amount of arguing or attempts to convince the people otherwise has the slightest effect.

To this manufactured town, their faces, their clothing, their mannerisms, all seem to be exactly what the Melkotians intend for them: to be the Clanton Gang, destined to die at five o'clock that afternoon.

One of them even dies *before* five: Chekhov, mistaken by a local girl for her lover Billy Clanton, is shot dead by Morgan Earp in a standoff over Sylvia's affections.

(Or IS he? More to come ...)

As the men mourn Chekhov's death, they are also at work creating a possible weapon imagined by Spock and McCoy: a tranquilizing gas grenade, with which they hope to immobilize the Earps long enough to either resolve or escape the situation. McCoy brings his extensive chemical and medical knowledge to bear, and he creates a perfect, scientifically proven, guaranteed effective tranquilizer.

Which *doesn't work.*

WHAT??

It's Spock who finally begins to realize the truth:

> *"It did not function ... but it MUST function. A scientific fact. But if the tranquilizer does not function, which is clearly impossible, then a radical alteration of our thought patterns must be in order."*

What's he talking about? Let's look deeper ...

It's at this moment that Kirk, Spock, Scotty, and McCoy are forced to the OK Corral. All avenues of escape are cut off, and they realize that they will have to fight the Earps ... but the Earps are expert gunfighters. Our heroes have no chance!

Or don't they? And now, Spock explains why they *may not need to fight at all.*

I mean, Doctor, that we are faced with a staggering contradiction.

The tranquilizer you created should have been effective...

Physical laws simply cannot be ignored.

Existence cannot be, without them.

Now, it gets REALLY deep.

Spock asks Dr. McCoy's opinion of what killed Chekhov. When "Bones" cites "a piece of lead in his body," Spock corrects him:

SPOCK: *Wrong. His MIND killed him.*

McCOY: *What do you mean unreal? I examined Chekhov - he's dead!*

SPOCK: *But you made your examination under conditions which we cannot trust. ... Physical reality is consistent with universal laws. Where the laws do not operate, there is no reality. All of this (the situation) is unreal. ...*

We judge reality by the response of our senses. Once we are convinced of the reality of a given situation, we abide by its rules. We judged the bullets to be solid, the guns to be real; therefore they can kill.

What is Spock talking about? Kirk now gives us a clue:

KIRK: *If we do not believe that the bullets are real, they cannot kill us!*

SPOCK: *Exactly. I know the bullets are unreal, therefore they cannot harm me.*

KIRK: *We must all be as certain as you are, Spock, if we're to save our lives.*

When McCoy admits that with humans, "there'd always be some doubt," Spock gets to the crux of the matter:

SPOCK: *THE SMALLEST DOUBT WOULD BE ENOUGH TO KILL YOU.*

McCOY: *We're just human beings, Spock. We don't have that clockwork ticker in our heads like you do. We can't just turn it on and off!*

KIRK: *We must. Spock: The Vulcan Mind Meld.*

What Kirk is referring to is an ancient Vulcan mental discipline called the Mind Meld, where a Vulcan joins his mind and thoughts to that of another, and thus can not only read, but influence the other's thought patterns.

Have you ever wished that you could control your thoughts, shut out unwanted influences and opinions, keep your "eyes on the prize" to the exclusion of all else?

Observe as Spock "mind-melds" with Scotty, McCoy, and Kirk – and shows their minds the truth about the illusory "threat" they face:

Your mind to my mind, your thoughts to
my thoughts. …
The bullets are unreal. Without body.
They are illusions only.
Shadows without substance.
They will not pass through your body,
for they do not exist.
Unreal. Appearances only.
They are shadows. Illusions.
Nothing but ghosts of reality.
They are lies. Falsehoods.
Spectres without body.
They are to be ignored.

Thus mentally fortified, the four men face off against the ephemeral Earps – and they emerge unharmed.

Our heroes are then transported back to the *Enterprise* – where they find Chekhov sitting at his station, alive and well. It seems Spock was right all along: even the "bullets" were unreal.

Small additional point here:

In this final shootout, Kirk is forced to defend himself in hand-to-hand combat – but when he gains the upper hand and has the chance to kill one of the Earps with his gun, Kirk refuses, and he spares the man's life.

The Melkotian notices this, and he asks Kirk about it:

> *"Captain Kirk, you did not kill. Is this the way of your kind?"*

Kirk confirms that "our mission is still one of peace," and the Melkotians agree to the beginning of treaty negotiations.

(What's the point? Just this: never respond to your critics in kind; stand your ground and stick to your purpose. In time, you may find that some will not be critics forever.)

Lesson You Can Use:

What are we trying to say here? That if you just "believe," you, too, can dodge bullets?

Of course not - nothing of the kind. However, Spock's reading of the truth beneath the illusion shows us that the slings and arrows of criticism, the doubt of others, and our own fears and insecurities can be overcome by applying our own form of "mind control" ... that is, by developing a superior state of mind, one that is built on positive expectation and the rejection of negative influences.

For specific tips and techniques on creating your OWN "Vulcan Mind Meld," I commend you to two classic works in the arts and science of personal development:

Think And Grow Rich, by Napoleon Hill

and

The Science of Getting Rich, by Wallace D. Wattles

There are hosts of others, of course – but I think these two are a pretty good place to start.

Remember, you're looking for the means and methods to "bulletproof" your mindset against the enemies of fear, insecurity, and disbelief.

The smallest doubt would be enough to kill you ... your *dreams,* that is.

Now, let's talk about one way to fight negative forces and obstacles to our success ... by *not fighting them at all.*

Chapter 4

"The More You Resist"

Franchise: The Original Series AND
The Next Generation
Season 3 (TOS), episode 12: "The Empath"
Season 7 (TNG), episode 4: "Gambit, Part 2"

We're going to take scenes, from two different episodes in the two different series, to illustrate one idea: That it is often possible to defeat our obstacles by not resisting them at all. It is in these calm, non-combative moments when we discover that what we thought was holding us back is not only not holding us back ... maybe it wasn't there at all.

In "The Empath," Kirk and crew are dispatched to evacuate a planet in the path of a coming supernova before the planet becomes uninhabitable.

When they arrive, Kirk, Spock, and McCoy are captured by the Vaians, a race populating one of the endangered planets. They also encounter a beautiful, silent woman from a race of mutes, who lives on another of the planets.

They soon discover that she is also an "empath" - in this case, the term meaning a being capable of connecting to and taking on the emotional and physiological responses of another. She demonstrates this by, in one instance, healing a head injury suffered by Captain Kirk; and in another, by taking onto herself the results of catastrophic, life-threatening experimental tortures inflicted on "Bones" McCoy by the Vaians.

The Vaians are seeking to determine whether Gem's (as Bones has come to call her) race are "worthy" of rescue from the planetary disaster about to befall them. To their minds, she can only do this by demonstrating the same compassion and courage for self-sacrifice shown by the three Starfleet officers, who each offer themselves to submit to horrible medical torture in order to protect the others.

When Gem passes their "test," the Vaiains release Kirk and his officers and disappear. Kirk, Spock, and McCoy return to the *Enterprise,* and they remark upon the awe-some power of the character they have witnessed in Gem.

The episode is interesting for several reasons; however, for me the key principle is illustrated in two separate scenes that I've not yet even mentioned ... they all have to do with *force fields.* Let's look at them in a bit more detail.

On the first of these three occasions, Kirk, Spock, and McCoy are seized and held captive in a Vaian-manufactured force field. Kirk struggles to free himself, barely able to stand. Dr. McCoy advises against it:

> **McCOY**: *Don't fight the force field - there's something about it that upsets the body metabolism.*

One of the Vaians clarifies:

> **LAL**: *Not quite, Doctor. The field draws its energy FROM your bodies. The more you resist, the stronger the force field becomes.*

Do you see it yet?

In another "force field" moment, Kirk and Spock are held in a force field, which Kirk again attempts to push through:

> **SPOCK**: *Captain, the intensity of emotion is draining us, and building up the force field. ... it draws its energy from us, Captain. In spite of what we see, all emotion must be suppressed. That might weaken the field ...*

And Spock, employing his renowned Vulcan mental discipline, clears his mind of all emotional response – and almost instantly, he lifts his hand ... and the force field simply vanishes.

Kirk requires an additional moment, but his power over his own mind is formidable as well, and he also escapes. Actually, he not so much escapes as he simply *releases his struggle* ... and for him, the force field also falls away.

Seeing the principle NOW?

It is simply this: When Kirk and Spock ceased to struggle against what they *thought* was a field blocking their path, the block – *which was generated by their own bodies and emotions in the first place* – disappeared almost as if by magic.

The same "art of fighting without fighting" is illustrated in the *Next Generation* episode cited here, "Gambit."

U.S.S. Enterprise Captain Jean-Luc Picard, thought by his crew to be dead, is in reality engaged in an undercover mission to recover a dangerous Vulcan weapon called a "psionic resonator."

The word *psionic* is defined by Webster as "relating to or denoting the practical use of psychic powers or paranormal phenomena." You can probably predict its interest to a group of violent Vulcan isolationists – it could be used to amplify aggressive emotions, and to turn them back to destroy the aggressor.

As the search for the resonator progresses, it develops that the old device has three glyphs, or sets of markings, carved into it: one depicts the ancient Vulcan goddess of War, one the god of Death. But because the resonator's assembly is not yet complete, the third glyph is missing.

When the isolationist leader, a Vulcan woman named T'Lera, recovers the missing piece and completes the weapon, using it to kill two of her former co-conspirators, Picard makes a momentous discovery:

> **PICARD**: *I can see the symbol on the third artifact – and it is the Vulcan symbol for Peace, standing between the symbols for War and Death.*
>
> *It's a warning that the power of the resonator can be overcome by peace.*

T'Lera attempts to use the resonator on Picard and his crew; however, having divined the device's operating dynamics, Picard and his crew empty their minds in that moment of all violent thoughts and make no aggressive movements, and we watch as the terrible shock waves emanating from the resonator pass harmlessly over their bodies.

The weapon is retrieved and destroyed; and order and peace are maintained on Vulcan, one of the founding worlds of the United Federation of Planets.

And there it is AGAIN: that release of resistance, that cease from struggle against INTERNAL conflict, that causes the seemingly irresistible external force to simply pass out of existence.

Now, this is by no means intended to suggest that all we have to do is "relax" and success will just show up.

We've still got to do our part – set our goal, formulate a plan to reach it, and then execute that plan consistently and in the full confidence that our efforts will eventually bear fruit.

What it DOES mean is that, though we may still need to fight through many challenges as we work to achieve what we want, we can save ourselves time, extra effort, and wasted mental energy by not fighting *ourselves* as well.

Lesson You Can Use

The toughest battle you will wage is *inside yourself.*

Find your inner calm, your own place of "non-resistance." Practice meditation, prayer, or other mindfulness exercises.

Once you have dropped your own "force field," the forces of others can no longer stand in your way.

Chapter 5

Two Words

Franchise: The Original Series
Season 3, Episode 19: "Requiem For Methuselah"

There are two words that have the power to make you freer, more alive, more fully HUMAN than any two other words in the English language.

Do you know what those words are? *Star Trek* has the answer …

Captain's log, stardate 5843.7.

The Enterprise is in the grip of a raging epidemic. Three crewmen have died and twenty-three others have been struck down by Rigelian fever.

In order to combat the illness, Doctor McCoy needs large quantities of ryetalyn, which is the only known antidote for the fever.

> Our sensors have picked up sufficient quantities of pure ryetalyn on a small planet in the Omega system. We are beaming down to secure this urgently needed material.

Immediately upon beaming down, Kirk, Spock, and McCoy meet a man named Flint, who welcomes them into his opulent home on the planet surface.

Noting the priceless – and previously unknown – works of art and music adorning Flint's mansion, the three men are greatly impressed … but Spock is beginning to sense that may not be as it seems. How could an unknown painting by da Vinci – which Spock confirms is authentic – have been painted with CONTEMPORARY canvas and materials?

The secret will soon be revealed … but in the meantime, Flint introduces the men to his ward, Rayna Kapec, who he says he took in following the death of her parents.

Rayna is young, brilliant, and beautiful, and of course, Kirk finds her irresistible. (What is it with Jim Kirk and alien women??)

In the course of securing the ryetalyn and synthesizing it for administration to the ailing *Enterprise* crew, Kirk, Spock, and Bones make two chilling discoveries: one, that

Flint is of immense age – virtually immortal; and the other, that Rayna is not actually his ward … indeed, she is not even human. She is an android:

FLINT: *Created here by my hand. Here, the centuries of loneliness were to end.*

SPOCK: *Your collection of Leonardo da Vinci masterpieces, Mister Flint, they appear to have been recently painted on contemporary canvas with contemporary materials. And on your piano, a waltz by Johannes Brahms, an unknown work in manuscript, written in modern ink. Yet absolutely authentic, as are your paintings.*

FLINT: *I am Brahms.*

SPOCK: *And da Vinci?*

FLINT: *Yes.*

SPOCK: *How many other names shall we call you?*

FLINT: *Solomon, Alexander, Lazarus, Methuselah, Merlin, Abramson. A hundred other names you do not know.*

Flint explains that he was born on Earth over 6,000 years before, and soon discovered that through lifetime after lifetime, he simply could not die. So he has learned to conceal his secret, and he has used his vast wealth and centuries of acquired knowledge and skills to create, as Spock calls Rayna, "a perfect, ultimate woman, as brilliant, as immortal as yourself. Your mate for all time."

Kirk, having by now fallen in love with Rayna, realizes that this is precisely what Flint had planned all along: to have Kirk use his charms to woo and romance Rayna, and somehow stir her android emotions to life, so that she would then turn to Flint in love.

But how will Flint rid himself of Kirk and the others? By imprisoning them, and the ship, in suspended animation, to be released

> *... in time. A thousand, two thousand years. You will know the future, Captain Kirk.*

Unacceptable to Kirk, of course. As is Flint's callous plan simply to use Kirk and then dispose of him. Kirk would have Rayna come with him, to join him on the *Enterprise*.

The men begin to fight. Rayna, who has come upon the scene and urged Flint not to imprison the crew, calls for them to cease fighting – and then, she utters the Two Words:

RAYNA: *I cannot be the cause of this. I will not be the cause of this.*

Please stop.

Stop!

I choose where I want to go, what I want to do.

I choose.

I choose.

FLINT: *Rayna!*

RAYNA: *No. Do not order me. No one can order me!*

KIRK: *She's human. Down to the last blood cell, she's human. Down to the last thought, hope, aspiration, emotion, she's human. The human spirit is free. You have no power of ownership. She's free to do as she wishes.*

Kirk begs Rayna to come with him; Flint begs her to stay. Her final words, uttered before she collapses, her circuitry overloaded by the conflicting data now coursing through it, are these:

I was not human.

Now I love. I love.

Lesson You Can Use:

… but did you catch the two words?

The two KEY words among Rayna's final words?

I choose.

What separates us from the rest of the animal kingdom? What gives us the ability to rise above our circumstances, to overcome any obstacle, to control our own emotions and our own responses to any and all situations?

Your freedom, your right – indeed, your responsibility – to choose.

You can choose what career direction you take. You can choose how you respond to the angry email in your inbox or the road-raging driver in the next lane. You can choose – first thing in the morning – what kind of day you're going to have.

And the moment you give up that choice, the moment you say "he *made* me upset" or "I *couldn't* help it" or "what was I *supposed to do?"* – in that moment, you become disempowered. At the effect, rather than the cause, of your life.

You become *less than fully human.*

Never surrender your free will to the push and pull of circumstance. Never allow someone else to exercise control over your emotions. Never give in to the thought that "I can't help it – that's just the way I am."

Stop. Take a breath. Realize that in every moment, the choice is yours, and yours alone.

Then … ***choose.***

Chapter 6

The First Duty

Franchise: The Next Generation
Season 5, Episode 19: "The First Duty"

When you're faced with a choice, under pressure, which do you choose:

Loyalty or principle?

We're about to take a look at how one young man nearly threw away his entire career by making the wrong choice.

What Happens:

The *Enterprise,* under the command of Captain Jean-Luc Picard, is on her way to Earth, where the Captain is scheduled to give the commencement address at the Starfleet Academy graduation ceremony.

Along the way, he is informed by Academy Superintendent Brand that an accident has befallen a beloved former crew member: Academy Cadet Welsey Crusher, the son of the *Enterprise's* Chief Medical Officer Dr. Beverly Crusher.

Fortunately, Wesley's injuries are not life-threatening … at least, not *physically.*

What do I mean? Well, it turns out that the accident took place during a practice run of a supposedly routine precision flying maneuver led by Wesley's classmate and "Nova Squadron" leader Nicholas Locarno - a crash that claimed the life of a fellow cadet.

During the investigation into the cause of the crash, the senior officers conducting the inquiry become suspicious that the members of Nova Squadron are not revealing all that they know about the circumstances. Even Wesley himself lied to the board of inquiry about aspects and specific details of the accident.

Why? Well, it's clear that Nick Locarno exerts a powerful mental and emotional influence over the other members of the squadron. He has convinced them not only to conceal the truth, but to blame the accident on Josh Albert, the cadet who was killed.

What's going on here? Captain Picard knows …

After conducting his own investigation, the Captain concludes that Nova Squadron was not in fact flying a routine maneuver, but was attempting a much more difficult and dangerous stunt, one intended to dazzle the viewers at the ceremony.

Picard confronts Wesley in the Captain's "Ready Room" (his private office near the main bridge) with the results of his investigation, and with his description of the dangerous "Kolvoord Starburst" maneuver:

> **PICARD**: *Five ships crossing within ten meters of each other and igniting their plasma trails. One of the most spectacular and difficult demonstrations of precision flying. It hasn't been performed at the Academy team in over a hundred years. Do you know why?*
>
> **WESLEY**: *It was banned by the Academy following a training accident, sir.*
>
> **PICARD**: *An accident in which all five cadets lost their lives.*
>
> *I think that Nicholas Locarno wanted to end his Academy career in a blaze of glory.*
>
> *That he convinced the four of you to learn the Kolvoord Starburst for the commencement demonstration.*

> *If it worked, you would thrill the assembled guests and Locarno would graduate as a living legend. Only it didn't work, and Joshua Albert paid the price.*
>
> *Am I correct?*
>
> *Cadet, I asked you a question! Am I correct?*
>
> *Incredibly, Wesley "chooses not to answer."*
>
> **PICARD**: *You choose not to answer? But you've already given an answer to the inquiry, and that answer was a lie.*
>
> **WESLEY**: *I said the accident occurred after the loop. It did.*
>
> **PICARD**: *But what you neglected to mention was that following the loop your team attempted a maneuver that was the direct cause of the crash. ... You told the truth up to a point. But a lie of omission is still a lie.*

Picard recalls Wesley's first visit to the main bridge, brought there as a child by his mother. Picard could see even then that Wesley had a remarkable knowledge of ship's system and operations, and:

> *And then later when I decided to make you an acting ensign, I was convinced you could be an outstanding officer.*
>
> *And I've never questioned that conviction ...*

... until now.

The first duty of every Starfleet officer is to the TRUTH!

Whether it's scientific truth, or historical truth, or personal truth. It is the guiding principle upon which Starfleet is based.

If you can't find it within yourself to stand up and tell the truth about what happened, you don't deserve to wear that uniform.

I'm going to make this simple for you, Mister Crusher. Either you come forward and tell Admiral Brand what really took place, or I will.

There it is. There's the heart of the matter. Picard makes known to Wesley, in no uncertain terms, that PRINCIPLE TRUMPS LOYALTY. It must, or else the very foundation of Starfleet's mission will collapse.

Wesley finally does realize the error of his choice. He admits to the inquiry what the squadron did; their punishment is swift and stern - Locarno even resigned from the Academy altogether.

But Wesley does retain his place at the Academy. He eventually graduates, and he is commissioned to serve in

Starfleet. And I believe the reason his career survived is that when the moment of truth came, he told the truth.

Lesson You Can Use:

I know of a certain direct sales company that has as one of its guiding principles the following: "The TRUTH Is Good Enough."

How many careers ... companies ... marriages ... political campaigns ... business ventures ... have been derailed, disgraced, destroyed ... because someone lied, or even shaded the truth, for the sake of convenience, or short-term gain, or self-preservation?

If you're a consultant, tell your clients the truth, even when they don't like it – they'll respect your forthrightness.

If you're having an intimate conversation, tell your friend the truth, even when she doesn't want to hear it – believe it or not, she'll thank you later.

If you're in sales, tell your prospect the truth, even if it costs you the sale – actually, it might NOT cost you the sale!

If you're in network marketing, quit it with the "miracle-cure" jive and the hyped-up income claims – only the gullible will believe you anyway. And the recruits you really want – the recruits you really NEED in your business – won't be scared away by the truth.

Just tell the truth ... it'll make your life a lot less complicated. As some wag has said, "if you always tell the truth, you don't need a good memory."

Chapter 7

OK, So You've Screwed Up. BIG Time. Now What?

Franchise: The Next Generation
Season 7, Episode 15: "Lower Decks"

It isn't often that a *Trek* episode is centered entirely around the lesser-known characters aboard the *Enterprise,* so this chapter/lesson is appealing on a couple of different levels.

First, we get a good look at life aboard a starship in places other than the bridge or the engine room – you may not know this, but the crew complement of a ship such as the *Enterprise* is over 1,000 members.

Also, as we'll see, there are important decisions being made – life-changing decisions – by crewmembers other than the iconic senior officers like Captain Picard, First Officer William Riker, or Tactical/Security Officer Worf (the only Klingon to serve aboard a Federation starship, with quite a story of his own).

What Happens:

It's Promotion Time.

First Officer Will Riker and his colleague and close friend, Ship's Counselor Deanna Troi, are reviewing performance evaluations and considering promotion recommendations for all ship's personnel. Their friendly banter speaks of a relationship that spans not only careers spent serving together, but a deep personal relationship.

It develops that two junior officers are up for promotion to the same job: Operations Officer, one of the senior bridge positions - a role which also comes with a rank upgrade from Ensign to Lieutenant.

The two officers in line are Ensign Sam Lavelle and Ensign Sito Jaxa. Lavelle is an eager young man originally from Canada, and Sito is …

… wait, you don't REMEMBER Sito Jaxa??

Oh! Well, let me refresh your memory …

Bajoran-born Sito Jaxa *(Trek Trivia Alert: In keeping with traditional Bajoran culture, she is addressed family name first, much as Chinese names are traditionally written today)* was one of the members of Wesley Crusher's Nova Squadron at the Academy.

Remember now? Yes, that's right – she was implicated in the coverup surrounding the training accident and death of another cadet. Punished and humiliated, she also managed to survive and graduate, just like Wesley, and she is now posted on the *Enterprise.*

She has performed admirably in her duties aboard ship, but Captain Picard appears singularly unimpressed, and he says so in a private Ready Room conversation with Sito:

> **PICARD**: *How long have you served on board the Enterprise, Ensign?*
>
> **SITO**: *Seven months, sir.*
>
> **PICARD**: *I see. I understand that you've been recommended for the Ops position. Do you think you're up to it?*
>
> **SITO**: *I do, sir.*
>
> **PICARD**: *I'm not so sure. I'm concerned about your record.*
>
> **SITO**: *Sir?*

PICARD: *The incident that you were involved in at the Academy.*

SITO: *With all due respect that was three years ago. My record since then –*

PICARD: *It doesn't matter how long ago it was, Ensign. Would you do something like that again?*

SITO: *I can assure you, sir, that I would never, never jeopardize lives by participating in –*

PICARD: *A daredevil stunt? I would certainly hope not. What concerns meis that you participated in a cover-up that impeded an official investigation into the death of a cadet.*

SITO: *Sir, I know I should have told the truth right from the start –*

PICARD: *Yes you should, but you didn't. Instead, you joined with the others to pretend that was simply an accident. Now, what do you think that tells me about your character?*

SITO: *Sir, if you had any idea what it was like after that incident. I didn't have any friends. I didn't have anyone to talk to. I had to take my flight test with the instructor because no one else would be my partner. In a lot of ways,* *it would have been easier to just walk away, but I didn't. I stuck with it. Doesn't that say something about my character, too?*

PICARD: *Well, I'm really very sorry you didn't enjoy your time at the Academy, Ensign. As far as I'm concerned, you should have been expelled for what you did. Quite frankly, I don't know how you made it on board this ship. You're dismissed.*

So, Sito's stained reputation has followed her to the flagship of the Fleet. What to do?

Well, it seems that Jaxa (we're all friends now, aren't we? First-name basis for sure!) already has her answer inside – at least, she's reminded of the answer by Worf, her immediate commanding officer, who recommended her for the promotion in the first place.

Following one of his Klingon martial arts classes, Worf invites Sito to undergo the *Gik'tal* challenge, to determine whether she is ready for more advanced studies. As a preparation for the challenge, Worf blindfolds Sito and challenges her to "defend yourself!"

Of course, she is completely disadvantaged; after being tripped and thrown several times by Worf, she rips the blindfold off:

SITO: *How am I supposed to defend myself when I can't see a thing?*

WORF: *Stop making excuses! Replace the blindfold!*

SITO: *No! It's not a fair test!*

WORF: *Very good, Ensign. You have passed the challenge.*

SITO: *What? By taking off the blindfold?*

WORF: *It takes courage to say the test is unfair.*

SITO: *One thing I don't understand. Doesn't gik'tal mean "to the death"?*

WORF: *You speak Klingon.*

SITO: *... Sir, is there really such a thing as a gik'tal challenge?*

WORF: *No, there is not.*

But perhaps next time you are judged unfairly, it will not take so many bruises for you to protest.

Thus reminded, and encouraged, Sito requests a second audience and returns to the Captain's Ready Room:

SITO: *All I've ever wanted is to make a career for myself in Starfleet. I can't change what happened at the Academy.*

No one can. All I can do is work hard and try to earn the respect of the people I serve with. If you're not going to give me that chance, then I respectfully request that you transfer me to another ship.

PICARD: *If you're looking for a more lenient commander, I don't think you'll find one.*

SITO: *Permission to speak freely, sir?*

PICARD: *Please do.*

SITO: *If you didn't want me on your ship, you should have said so when I was assigned to it. It's not your place to punish me for what I did at the Academy. I've worked hard here. My record is exemplary. If you're going to judge me, judge me for what I am now.*

PICARD: *Very well, Ensign. I will.*

It took courage to come here and face me after what I said to you the other day. I didn't ask you here because I was assessing your qualifications for the Ops position.

SITO: *I don't understand, sir.*

PICARD: *I was harsh with you because I wanted to assess you for a very important mission. A mission that could put* *you in a situation that would be far more unnerving than a dressing-down by your commanding officer.*

SITO: *Can I ask what that mission is, sir?*

PICARD: *Join the senior officers in the Observation Lounge at oh-nine-hundred hours (9:00 am to us non-military types). We'll discuss it then.*

SITO: *Yes, sir.*

PICARD: *And, Ensign, I do know why you ended up on the Enterprise.*

I asked for you.

I wanted to make sure that you got a fair chance to redeem yourself.

SITO: *Thank you, sir.*

Lesson You Can Use:

Now, you and I may not have the good fortune to be led by someone so willing to give US another chance to redeem ourselves after we've screwed up … and trust me: you *will* screw up. More than once, I'll wager.

But here's what I do know: Ensign Sito was willing to stake her continuing service on the *Enterprise,* indeed her entire Starfleet career, on the quality of her work since the scandal that derailed her. She didn't let the mistakes of the past keep her from giving 100% of her effort to the present.

And, finally, the right person noticed – and gave her another chance.

And you can bet she took advantage of that second chance.

Will you?

Are you willing to bet your job, your business, your future, on the quality of your work TODAY – even after a mistake that seemed so disastrous at the time, you thought you'd ruined everything?

Or will you give up?

Will you throw up your hands and say, "Oh, what's the use? I've ruined everything - I've missed my chance!"

Will you *choose* – there's that word again – to release the guilt of your past, and to rededicate yourself to excellence ... in THIS moment? Which, after all, is the only thing you can control anyway?

By the way, the mission of which the Captain spoke was indeed an extremely dangerous one – and it was a mission that our friend young Sito Jaxa completed with distinction:

> **PICARD**: *To all Starfleet personnel, this is the Captain.*
>
> *It is my sad duty to inform you that a member of the crew, Ensign Sito Jaxa, has been lost in the line of duty.*
>
> *She was the finest example of a Starfleet officer, and a young woman of remarkable courage —* ***and strength of character.***
>
> *Her loss will be deeply felt by all who know her.*
>
> *Picard out.*

Chapter 8

"Risk Is Our Business"

Franchise: The Original Series
Season 2, Episode 20: "Return To Tomorrow"

This episode, though perhaps less well-known, contains what may be one of the most iconic speeches in *Trek* history – and it certainly communicates a priceless lesson for anyone in the business of personal achievement.

What Happens:

A distress signal from an unidentified source draws the *Enterprise* to a planet far beyond where any other starship has thus far explored. Captain Kirk and crew are invited by the seemingly disembodied voice of "Sargon" to enter orbit about the planet, and to transport down several very specific personnel: Kirk, Spock, McCoy, and a crew-member named Dr. Ann Mulhall.

Once landing on the planet, the Captain and crew learn Sargon's intent. He is indeed without physical form –

only the essence of his intellect remains, housed in a globe-like receptacle, from which he has been "searching the heavens with my mind" for a ship to assist him.

He is from a race and culture many thousands of centuries older than that of Earth, highly intelligent and technologically advanced, who have nonetheless destroyed themselves in war. Only three inhabitants remain, essences enclosed in the receptacles: Sargon, his wife Thalesa, and Hannok, a member of the "other side" in their planet's cataclysmic battle.

Sargon's request: to "borrow" the bodies of Kirk, Spock, and Ann Mulhall for a short time, by inserting their essences into them. They wish to do this in order to have the use of their human hands, to construct "robot bodies" which they would then inhabit and thus "live again."

Sargon does not force this choice on Kirk or the crew; he leaves them to come to a decision freely, and he assures Kirk that the three aliens will respect whatever decision they make.

In a conference room back aboard the *Enterprise,* all the parties involved are discussing what to do. Kirk, Spock, McCoy, and Ann Mulhall are there, along with Chief Engineer Scott, who will be working closely with the aliens in the construction process.

Kirk and Spock share with the assembled group some of the remarkable advances possible by learning from the aliens' superior technologies, and it is indeed impressive; as Spock states, mankind could "leap forward ten thousand years."

"Bones" McCoy is understandably concerned at the obvious physical dangers:

> **KIRK**: *Bones? You could stop all this by saying no. That's why I called you all here together. We'll all be deeply involved. It must be unanimous.*
>
> **MCCOY**: *Then I'll still want one question answered to my satisfaction.*
>
> *Why?*
>
> *Not a list of possible miracles, but a simple basic understandable why that overrides all danger. And let's not kid ourselves that there is no potential danger in this.*

Then Captain James T. Kirk declares the entire purpose of Starfleet, of exploration ... indeed perhaps his whole reason for being.

> **KIRK**: *They used to say if man could fly, he'd have wings. But he did fly. He discovered he had to.*

Do you wish that the first Apollo mission hadn't reached the moon, or that we hadn't gone on to Mars and then to the nearest star? That's like saying you wish that you still operated with scalpels and sewed your patients up with catgut like your great-great-great-great-grandfather used to.

I'm in command. I could order this. But I'm not. Because Doctor McCoy is right in pointing out the enormous danger potential in any contact with life and intelligence as fantastically advanced as this.

But I must point out that the possibilities, the potential for knowledge and advancement is equally great.

Risk. Risk is our business!

That's what the starship is all about. That's why we're aboard her!

You may dissent without prejudice. Do I hear a negative vote?

(There's silence around the table.

... Would *you* dissent?)

Engineer, stand by to beam aboard three receptacles.

Thus the transference begins. The bodies of Kirk, Spock, and Ann are inhabited by the essences of Sargon, Hannok, and Thalesa, and construction of the robots commences.

However, Hannok proves to be as treacherous in Spock's body as he evidently was in his previous form. He attempts to murder Sargon (and, by extension, Kirk) and to convince Thalesa to keep the human forms they have appropriated, and in so doing to murder Spock and Ann as well.

Fortunately, Sargon has anticipated Hannok's treachery. He and other senior *Enterprise* officers manage to defeat and destroy Hannok; then he and Thalesa agree to vacate Kirk's and Ann's bodies and return to oblivion ... but not before a last, tender moment together in physical form (you didn't think we'd through an ENTIRE episode without Kirk kissing the girl, did you?).

Lesson You Can Use:

As a child, and even now, I never fail to be struck by the courage of James T. Kirk. His willingness to put himself, his ship, *everything,* on the line, to complete the mission, to defeat the enemy, to expand human knowledge and advancement, has always been a source of inspiration to me.

What's YOUR risky decision? What's the choice you know you need to make, but are hesitating to make because you fear the outcome may not be what you hope for?

Here's what I know: You'll never know what leaps you could make, what you might achieve, what heights may stand before you, if you don't even try.

As Wayne Gretzky, the greatest hockey player who ever lived, once said, "You'll miss 100% of the shots you don't take."

Risk is YOUR business!

Chapter 9

Furry Object Syndrome

Franchise: The Original Series
Season 2, Episode 15: "The Trouble With Tribbles"

Hey, entrepreneurs! Small business owners! Network marketing professionals!

No, not over there - look over HERE!

And now that I have your attention:

Did you know that it's possible to cripple your entire mission, halt everything you're trying to accomplish, miss goal after goal, risk running your whole business into the ground ...

... and not even realize you're doing it?

Yup. and the warning signs are hidden in this delightful little dollop of all-time *Trek* comedy.

By the way, you're not going to get a lot of detailed descriptions of this episode here. The reason is that, if you've never watched *Star Trek* before, if you've never before taken the time to get acquainted with these legendary characters, I think you ought to make this episode your introduction to the *Trek* universe.

I've seen people who aren't fans – heck, I've seen people who've never seen a SINGLE episode before – beside themselves laughing at the hijinks herein.

Yes, that's right:

You're going to have to *go watch this one yourself.*

And now with that out of the way, a few pointers:

The *Enterprise* is summoned to Space Station K7 on an urgent distress call. In fact, as Captain Kirk puts it in his log:

> Captain's Log, stardate 4523.3. Deep Space Station K7 has issued a Priority One call. More than an emergency, it signals near or total disaster. We can only assume the Klingons have attacked the station. We're going in armed for battle.

What they find isn't a battle with the Klingons, the sworn enemies of the Federation. In fact, they don't meet a battle at all ... they meet a bureaucrat. Nilz Barris, a preening government functionary from the Federation. Arrogant, pretentious, issuing ridiculously nonsensical orders ... I imagine you've seen the type before.

He isn't the worst of the trouble, though. Nor are the Klingons. The worst of it – in fact, the thing that truly disrupts not only the station, but the *Enterprise* and the Klingon ship as well – is the appearance of the creatures in question.

The TRIBBLES.

Soft, fuzzy, furry, purry little pets that are so sweet, so soothing, and so impossibly CUTE, that they nearly bring the entire STARSHIP to a grinding halt!

How in the heck do they do THAT, you say?

Like I said before:

Watch. The. Episode.

But here's the ***Lesson You Can Use:***

Ever been fired up to get things done? Excited about accomplishing boatloads of work in or on your business? Ready to attack the phone and bang out that ton of follow-up calls you've been meaning to make?

… and then you look up an hour and a half later, and you *haven't done a damn thing??*

OK, how'd that happen? I'll tell you how:

Distractions.

The phone rings.

Your assistant comes into the office with a question.

Your roommate comes into the apartment with a pizza.

There's a knock at the door.

The pot on the stove boils over.

The movie playing on the TV hits a dramatic climax.

Your computer dings with that email from your buddy.

Your computer dings with that email from your BOSS.

You see an ad for a business that "looks SO much better" than the one you're building now.

You just wanna get this ONE Facebook post finished …

… and ninety minutes have flown by and you're scrolling kitten videos again or nodding and shouting Amen! to another political rant and now you've missed your goal or dropped your deadline or blown your project or you've left your network marketing company completely for the "greener grass" someplace else and WHY DOES THIS KEEP HAPPENING TO ME ....

So, how to prevent it?

Actually, the better question is WHY to prevent it?

As in, stop. Turn your phone off (yes, I went there – turn it OFF). Close the door to your room or your office. Shut out everything - EVERYTHING - for fine minutes – then sit quietly and ask yourself:

What's my WHY?

Why am I doing this in the first place?

What's my goal? What am I shooting for?

And is it important enough to me that I'm willing to put aside everything else for the next FIVE MINUTES and work ONLY on this task that will move me closer to my goal?

I know, I know – I only said five minutes. But you've been fighting this distraction thing a long time, haven't you? You've been derailed more than once, haven't you?

You've switched companies for what you *thought* was a better deal before, right? Maybe a few times? (In the network marketing game it's called "shiny object syndrome" … see what I did there?)

So, to begin to overcome your distractibility, let's start with FIVE minutes. Just five. Make one call. Complete one task. Write one paragraph or one page. Answer one email. Get one thing done – really done.

Then stop again, and CONGRATULATE yourself. You did it! Well done!

Now see if you can do it again, for another five minutes.

And then maybe ten minutes.

Wanna try for 15?

And before you know it, ninety minutes, ninety days have passed – and you look up and your goal is in your rearview mirror.

Just gotta get the tribbles off the bridge first ...

Chapter 10

"Let's Get The Hell Out Of Here"

Franchise: The Original Series
Season 1, Episode 28: "The City On The Edge of Forever"

To legions of old-school fans, this is the definitive *Trek* episode, the standard by which all others are judged.

It's got time travel.

It's got humor.

It's got suspense.

It's got *Joan Collins,* for crying out loud!

... AND it's got a powerful lesson, one to never be forgotten or overlooked:

The most important choice you make is usually the toughest.

And it's going to cost you.

Onward ...

In orbit around a new planet, the *Enterprise* encounters unusual and extreme turbulence, which Spock describes thusly:

> *Captain, this is of great scientific importance: we are actually passing through ripples in time.*

A sudden electrical accident injures the ship's helmsman, Lt. Hikaru Sulu, prompting a call from the bridge for Dr. McCoy. He arrives and, seeing Sulu's condition, administers a small dose of a powerful heart drug called *cordrazine;* it immediately revives Sulu and returns him to health.

Another turbulent jolt rocks the bridge, causing "Bones" to accidentally inject himself with over 100 times the small amount that revived Sulu, sending him into a wild, paranoid mania.

He flees the bridges, eludes a security search, and manages to transport himself down to the planet's surface. Kirk, along with Spock, Scott, Uhura, and a security detail follow him down.

Once there, Kirk and Spock discover the source of the waves of time displacement: The *Guardian of Forever,* an ancient yet highly advanced object which has the ability to "replay" all of history for display to the viewer.

McCoy is captured and subdued; meanwhile, Kirk and Spock suddenly consider the possibility of "turning back time" to just before the incident on the bridge, in hopes of avoiding McCoy's hypo accident.

Suddenly, however, Bones awakes, slips through their grasp, and leaps into the *Guardian.* At that moment, the landing party loses all contact with the Enterprise. The *Guardian* informs them that because McCoy has somehow changed history,

> *Your ship, your world – all that you knew is gone.*

Kirk and Spock decide to go back in time as well, in an attempt to set right whatever McCoy had changed. Their "leap back" lands them in 1930's Depression-era New York City, where they end up in the 21st Street Mission and encounter its administrator, Sister Edith Keeler (yes, you guessed it: the beauteous Joan Collins). Of course, Kirk is smitten almost immediately, but there's something he doesn't yet know.

Kirk and Spock have been using Spock's tricorder (an advanced analysis and recording device) to try to pinpoint the "focal point in time" – that is, the thing that McCoy changed that seems to have altered all history. Spock finally uncovers the truth:

Edith Keeler IS the focal point.

What soon becomes clear is that in order to set things right, what must happen is the unthinkable:

> **KIRK**: *Spock, I believe I'm in love with Edith Keeler.*
>
> **SPOCK**: *Jim, Edith Keeler … must die.*

Spock informs Kirk from his research of history that Edith Keeler will be killed in some sort of traffic accident – and the moment of truth soon arrives.

Kirk and Spock finally find McCoy, and there is a moment's joyful reunion. But then Edith approaches to meet them – *walking across a crowded street* – and Kirk knows. It's time.

McCoy sees the car speeding toward Edith and he tries to dash into the street to save her – and Kirk STOPS him.

> **MCCOY**: *You deliberately stopped me, Jim. I could have saved her. Do you know what you just did??!*

SPOCK: *He knows, Doctor. He knows.*

And in that moment, the pain, the torment on Kirk's face tells the story.

He has saved the galaxy. He has righted all of human history.

And ... he has sacrificed his love to do it.

The three are instantly transported back to the Guardian's planet to rejoin the landing party. All is well. The *Enterprise* signals, ready to beam them back up.

And in response to their query, Kirk, for the first and only time in the entire Original Series, utters something close to an obscenity:

Let's get the hell out of here.

Lesson You Can Use:

Be prepared. No great achievement comes easily, or without cost.

You probably won't have to leave someone to die ... but you may need to let go of a longstanding relationship that no longer serves you, or a job that no longer supports your career goals, or a company that has fallen out of integrity, but where you've built a network of colleagues and friends.

The cost, at the time, may seem high; indeed, it may BE high. But I believe that the long-term benefit and growth awaiting you on the other side of that choice will far outweigh the temporary loss.

The key is, do YOU believe it?

EPILOGUE

"To Them And Their Posterity ..."

So we come to the end of this first journey together.

I suspect we'll be meeting again soon.

There are so many rich veins of wisdom contained in the legacy of *Star Trek* that, so many more guidelines for living today, so much more I want to share with you.

For now, let me leave you with this question:

What does *your* future – *your* "undiscovered country," as Shakespeare put it – look like?

In the last feature film to center around the original crew, *Star Trek VI: The Undiscovered Country,* Captain Kirk and the crew of the *Enterprise* are faced with what looks like the end of their journey:

The Klingon Empire, the mortal enemies of the United Federation of Planets, is forced by tragic circumstances to seek a truce with the Federation, and they sue for peace in the person of Gorkon, the Chancellor of the Klingon High Council.

Kirk and his ship are dispatched to escort Gorkon to a proposed peace conference on Earth ... an assignment which forces Kirk to recall a deep personal loss:

> Captain's log, stardate 9522.6. I've never trusted Klingons, and I never will.
>
> I can never forgive them for the death of my boy.
>
> ...
>
> To me, our mission to escort the Chancellor of the Klingon High Council to a peace summit ... is problematic, at best.
>
> Spock says this could be a historic occasion, and I'd like to believe him. But how on earth can history get past people like me?

A shocking assassination, and the betrayal that precipitated it, are part of a diabolical plot to bring the Federation and the Empire once again to the brink of interstellar war.

Captain Kirk and Dr. McCoy are convicted of murder in the assassination and are sentenced to a fate worse than death - life at hard labor on *Rura Penthe,* a brutal penal planet known throughout the galaxy as "The Aliens' Graveyard."

Once they make their daring escape (you knew they would, didn't you?), they rejoin Spock and crew aboard the Enterprise, and together they foil the plans of those who would disrupt the Federation-Klingon peace conference.

The culprits are captured, the conspirators are exposed, and the galaxy is brought a step closer to peace.

At the moment of resolution, Kirk addresses the conference attendees:

> *Some people think the future means the end of history.*
>
> *Well, we haven't run out of history just yet.*
>
> *People can be very frightened of change.*

I might make a comment here about the turbulent times during which this book was created. But then, it seems to me that throughout human history, ALL times have been turbulent times. War, disease, natural disasters of all kinds, disruption and upheaval in human affairs, have always placed challenges before us.

How shall we face and resolve the challenges of OUR time, and move forward together as a race?

How shall we learn to overcome our differences – indeed, to celebrate our differences – and, as Captain Kirk once said, *"each learn to be delighted with who we are?"*

Permit me, dear reader, to suggest a course of action:

First, let us embrace and build within ourselves the highest qualities demonstrated by the Captains and the crews of the *Enterprise* ...

- Truth
- Self-discipline
- Relentless hard work
- Respect for all – even for apparent adversaries
- Focus
- Courage
- Sacrifice
- Friendship

And then, once these ideals have become our way of living, have become the essence of who we are, let us dedicate ourselves to passing on the lessons we learn to those who will follow us on this journey aboard the third planet in our solar system.

It's been described in many ways ... "each one teach one" ... "pay it forward" ... "leave a legacy" ... but the core principle is the same:

The only mark we can make on this planet is the one we'll leave behind.

Or, as stated in these final words from Starfleet's greatest Captain, James Tiberius Kirk:

> Captain's Log, U.S.S. Enterprise, stardate 9529.1.
>
> This is the final cruise of the Starship Enterprise under my command.
>
> This ship and her history will shortly become the care of another crew.
>
> To them and their posterity will we commit our future.
>
> They will continue the voyages we have begun, and journey to all the undiscovered countries, boldly going where no man ...
>
> ... where no one ...
>
> ... has gone before.

Live long and prosper, my friend.

BIBLIOGRAPHY

Chapter 2: "Balance of Terror," TOS. Original Airdate: 15 Dec, 1966. Screenwriter: Paul Schneider.

Chapter 3: "Spectre Of The Gun," TOS. Original Airdate: October 25, 1968. Screenwriter: Gene L. Coon.

Chapter 4: Season 3, episode 12: "The Empath," TOS. Original Airdate: December 6, 1968. Screenwriter: Joyce Muskrat.

Season 7, episode 5: "Gambit, Part !!," TNG. Original Airdate: October 18, 1993. Screenwriter: Naren Shankar.

Chapter 5: Season 3 episode 19: "Requiem For Methuselah," TOS. Original Airdate: December 6, 1968. Screenwriter: Jerome Bixby.

Chapter 6: Season 3, episode 19: "The First Duty," TOS. Original Airdate: March 30, 1992. Screenwriter: Ronald D. Moore & Naren Shankar.

Chapter 7: Season 7, episode 12: "Lower Decks," TNG. Original Airdate: February 7, 1994. Screenwriter: Ronald Wilkerson & Jean Louise Matthias.

Chapter 8: Season 2, episode 20: "Return To Tomorrow," TOS. Original Airdate: February 9, 1968. Screenwriter: John T. Dugan.

Chapter 9: Season 2, episode 15: "The Trouble With Tribbles," TOS. Original Airdate: December 6, 1968. Screenwriter: Joyce Muskrat.

Chapter 10: Season 3, episode 12: "The City On The Edge Of Forever," TOS. Original Airdate: April 6, 1967. Screenwriter: Harlan Ellison.

Epilogue: "Star Trek VI: The Undiscovered Country," TOS cast. Original Theatrical Release Date: December 6, 1991. Screenwriters: Nicholas Meyer and Denny Martin Flinn. Story by Leonard Nimoy, Lawrence Konner and Mark Rosenthal.

Made in the USA
Middletown, DE
30 April 2022

Made in the USA
Middletown, DE
30 April 2022